THE
SEVEN WAYS
TO OVERCOME
THE FEDERAL
STATUTE OF
LIMITATIONS

Other books by Fourth Dimension

The Underground Credit Builder's Handbook – What You Need to Know to Build Personal and Business Credit Successfully

THE
SEVEN WAYS
TO OVERCOME
THE FEDERAL
STATUTE OF
LIMITATIONS

BY

FOURTH DIMENSION

Book design: Dean Fetzer, www.gunboss.com

Cover design: Gary McCluskey,
www.garymccluskey.carbonmade.com

"Diligence is the mother of good fortune, and idleness, its opposite, never led to good intention's goal."

—Cervantes, *Don Quixote (1605)*

Legal Disclaimer

WARNING: This book is intended for informational purposes only and is sold and/or distributed with the understanding that neither the author, publisher, licensee, seller, distributor, or copyright holder are licensed to, or engaged in, rendering legal, accounting, financial, or any other professional services or advice.

If legal, financial, or any other expert assistance is required, the purchaser/reader of this book should seek the services of a competent attorney or other relevant type of professional.

We are not responsible as to how you decide to use this information. This book has controversial ideas and themes and may not be well liked by the courts.

It is important to note that the law changes frequently and we cannot guarantee that this information is either accurate or current. In fact, this information should be double-checked through use of your own resources.

Always be wise and use diligence in all of your undertakings, especially when it comes to legal matters.

Contents

"Bad laws are the worst sort of tyranny."

—Edmund Burke, Speech at Bristol (1780)

Introduction

One of the greatest injustices of our legal system is the Federal Statute of Limitations.

These limitations are meant to represent the needs of the judicial system rather than the needs of the people dependent on the judicial system.

This book was written with the humble purpose of balancing the judicial system's so-called needs of finality, comity and conserving judicial resources with the people's need for legitimate recourse through the judicial system.

In this book you will see that, in rare circumstances, there are some exceptions to the rigid Federal Statute of Limitations.

Hopefully, the information contained within will help you along your way down the path to justice.

"Under a government which imprisons any unjustly, the true place for a just man is also a prison."

—Henry David Thoreau, *Civil Disobedience* (1849)

AEDPA

BEWARE: of the Antiterrorism and Effective Death Penalty Act ("AEDPA" hereafter). The AEDPA was enacted in 1996 when it was signed into law by then President William J. Clinton ("Bill"). See Pub. Law No. 104-132, 110 Stat. 1214 (1996).

The AEDPA was meant to make it difficult for a prisoner to use a habeas proceeding to challenge his sentence or conviction, and it does.

Possibly the worst thing that the AEDPA has done is that it has created a one-year time bar on post-conviction motions for relief. Basically, a person in prison has one year to learn everything there is to know about the law and his case and file his petition for relief before that year is up or he will be forever barred from raising those claims. This rule is known in short as the AEDPA time bar.

The AEDPA also created a more rigorous standard of review which made it even more difficult for a prisoner to get relief.

Hands down, the AEDPA has done more harm to prisoners seeking federal post-conviction relief than anything else in the history of our country.

So be sure to familiarize yourself with the AEDPA, because if you don't, you may overlook something critical and be forever barred.

"I am ashamed the law is such an ass."

—George Chapman, *Revenge for Honour* (1964)

PLRA

BEWARE: of the Prison Litigation Reform Act ("PLRA" hereafter). See, 28 U.S.C. § 1915.

Besides the statute of limitations, it is important to note that there are many other hurdles and pitfalls that a prisoner must watch out for or overcome in order to obtain federal civil relief.

Like its cousin the AEDPA, the PLRA was signed into law by Bill Clinton back in 1996. And it was also meant to impede a prisoner's access to the federal judicial system. It does.

The PLRA changed various parts of the United States Code in order to make it harder for a prisoner to file a civil complaint into federal court and obtain relief.

The PLRA has many provisions designed to limit a prisoners' success at obtaining meaningful relief. Some of the provisions are rules for administrative remedy exhaustion. A lot of the provisions are about a prisoner filing "in forma pauperis" (as a poor person). Yet this list of harmful provisions goes on and on and on...

Be wise and familiarize yourself with the PLRA. Because if you don't, you may overlook something critical and be forever barred.

4

"A precedent embalms a principle. "

—William Scott, Lord Stowell, *Opinion* (1788)

Types of Precedent

CAUTION: This book cites many authorities such as Supreme Court, Circuit Court, and District Court cases. This is why it is important for the reader to understand the differences between types of "precedent."

There happens to be many types of precedent (e.g. declatory, original, super precedent, binding, persuasive, etc.). But, the two types of precedent that are most relevant to the context of this book are "binding" and "persuasive."

Binding precedent is an authority that a court must follow. There's no discretionary choice involved when it comes to this type of precedent. For instance, the holding in a U.S. Supreme Court case is a binding precedent to all other courts in the United States.

Persuasive precedent is an authority that is not binding on a court, but that is entitled to respect and careful consideration. For instance, the holding in one Court of Appeals would only be persuasive precedent in another Court of Appeals.

It is important to note that in some very rare situations, one court may have adopted another court's holding as binding precedent. A good example of this is found in <u>Bonner v. City of Prichard</u>, 661 F.2d 1206, 1209 (en banc) where the Eleventh Circuit Court of Appeals adopted as "binding" precedent all of the decisions of the former Fifth Circuit Court of Appeals handed down prior to the close of business on September 30, 1981. This means that if you happen to be in a situation where you rely on case law out of the Eleventh Circuit Court of Appeals, you need to be sure that your research includes Fifth Circuit case law that was decided prior to the close of business on September 30, 1981.

This book may cite cases that are out of different districts and circuits than the one in which your case originates. These cases will not be considered as binding precedent if you cite them in your case. You must take these cases and try to find cases from your district or circuit that make the same points and cite them instead.

In some circumstances, your district or circuit may have taken a position contrary to the authority cited in this book. In this situation, you must try to distinguish your case from the one that they used to make their decision and instead liken it to the more favorable case outside your district or circuit.

"The Lord is my Shepard [to feed, guide, and shield me] I shall not lack."

—Psalm 23:1 (*Amplified Bible*)

Shepardizing

Whenever filing things into court, you must always try to ensure that the cases you are citing have not been overruled, reversed, or distinguished. It is very bad practice to just take someone's word for it or to cite a case without having checked on the status of its validity. I suggest you use Shepard's to check on it. "Shepard's Citations" ("Shepard's" hereafter) is a very important legal research tool used widely among the legal field. Shepard's provides a listing of all of the cases that have cited the case that you are checking on. When you use this tool to check on a case it is called "Shepardizing." I suggest that you Shepardize a case before you use it.

Please make sure that your research is up-to-date and always double-check your resources, including this book. Shepardizing is one of the best ways to do this, and Shepard's is found in most law libraries nowadays. Don't be afraid to ask a law clerk for help in using Shepard's if you have a difficult time in figuring it out for yourself.

As I pointed out previously in the section on "Types of Precedent," I may cite cases that are out of different districts or circuits than your case is out of. These cases will not be considered as binding precedent if you cite them in your case. Shepard's is a great tool for this reason because it can help you find a case out of your district or circuit that lines up with the case that you happen to rely on.

"Procrastination is the thief of time."

—Edward Young, *Night Thoughts* (1742-5)

Applicable Statute of Limitations

Whether it be a Civil suit, or a motion for post-conviction relief in a criminal case by way of collateral attack (e.g. 28 U.S.C. § § 2241, 2255, etc.), there are always going to be time bars set in place.

The statute of limitations is a time bar. For every case and situation a different statute of limitations will apply.

There is no way for me to identify or comment on the particular time bar in in your case because I don't have the facts of your case or situation in front of me. Furthermore, it is beyond the scope of this book to tackle all of the possible Federal Statute of Limitations for criminal and civil matters. The real goal of this book is to show you that there are at least seven ways to overcome the Federal Statute of Limitations. It is your duty to identify the applicable statute of limitations which you are going to have to overcome.

In this book I will show you the seven ways that I know of to overcome the Federal Statute of Limitations. Some of these ways apply only in criminal matters. Some of these ways apply in both criminal and civil matters. My objective here is to simply show you that these tools exist, it is your duty to research and develop them further to see if they have any application to your particular case.

For federal criminal post-conviction matters, I suggest that you first read the Federal Rules of Criminal Procedure along with 28 U.S.C. §§ 2241-2266.

For federal civil matters, I suggest that you first read the Federal Rules of Civil Procedure.

The Seven Ways to Overcome the Federal Statute of Limitations

"In former days, everyone found the assumption of innocence so easy; today we find fatally easy the assumption of guilt."

—Amanda Cross, *Poetic Justice* (1970)

I. Actual Innocence

The problem with the term "actual innocence" is that it is used too often with rarely enough clarity.

Criminal

Three Types of Actual Innocence Claims

The Eleventh Circuit Court of Appeals in <u>Rozzelle v. Sec'y Fla. Dept. of Corr.</u>, 672 F.3d 1000 (11th Cir. 2012), identified three different types of actual innocence claims:

In the first type of actual innocence claim, a petitioner's "free-standing" actual innocence is itself the Constitutional basis of the habeas petition. See e.g. <u>Herrera v. Collins</u>, 506 U.S. 390 (1993)(habeas relief is not available for free-standing non-capital habeas claims).

In the second type of actual innocence claim, a petitioner's actual innocence serves as a gateway to the consideration of his Constitutional claims that would otherwise be barred, e.g. Constitutional claims procedurally defaulted in state court; failure to exhaust state remedies; failure to satisfy state filing requirements; etc. See e.g. Johnson v. Alabama, 256 F.3d 1156 (11th Cir. 2001).

In the third type of actual innocence claim, a petitioner seeks to have his claims heard by showing "cause and prejudice." See e.g. Arthur v. Allen, 452 F.3d 1234 (11th Cir. 2006).

Constitutional Violation

For non-capital petitioners, "actual innocence" is not an affirmative claim upon which a habeas petition may be granted. Rather, it is an exception that allows a petitioner to overcome hurdles such as: the AEDPA's statute of limitations; defenses of abusive or successive use of the writ of habeas corpus; and the rule of procedural default.

Thus, a non-capital petitioner must show that his conviction is the result of a Constitutional violation. See e.g. Smith v. Murray, 477 U.S. 527, at 496 (1986).

New Evidence & No Reasonable Juror

Any petitioner, capital or non-capital, who is intent on invoking an actual innocence claim, must present "new" evidence that is reliable which has not been previously presented. Moreover, the petitioner must demonstrate that in light of this new evidence which has never been reviewed on its merits, no reasonable juror would vote to convict him. To say it simpler: would a reasonable juror vote to convict the petitioner in light of the new evidence? See e.g. Schlup v. Delo, 513 U.S. 298, 324-327 (1995).

Factual Innocence

It is important to note that "actual innocence" means factual innocence rather than mere legal innocence. See e.g. Bousley v. United States, 523 U.S. 614 (1998).

> **actual innocence**
> The absence of facts that are prerequisites for the sentence given to a defendant. id.
> —Black's Law Dict. (7th Ed.)

> **legal innocence**
> The absence of one or more procedural or legal bases to support the sentence given to a defendant.
> —Black's Law Dict. (7th Ed.)

Example of an Actual Innocence Claim

"A prototypical example of 'actual innocence' in a colloquial sense is the case where the state have convicted the wrong person of the crime." Sawyer v. Whiteley, 505 U.S. 333, 340 (1992).

Convicted of a Non-Existent Crime

A person who is convicted of a non-existent crime meets the definition of "actually innocent."

First, the Supreme Court in Davis v. United States, 417 U.S. 333, 346-47 (1974) made it perfectly clear that when a defendant's conviction and punishment are "for an act that the law does not make criminal," there can be no room for doubt that such circumstances inherently result in a "complete miscarriage of justice." id. Then, in Smith v. Murray, 477 U.S. 527, 537 (1986), the Supreme Court clarified that "the miscarriage of justice exception is concerned with actual as compared to legal innocence." id.

Thus, "a petitioner is actually innocent when he was convicted for conduct not prohibited by the law." Alaimalo v. United States, 645 F.3d 1042, 1047 (9th Cir. 2011). See also Reyes-Requena v. United States, 243 F.3d 893 (5th Cir. 2001) ("because his claim is that he has been imprisoned for non-criminal conduct...he meets the actual innocence prong..." id.); and, Jennings v. Quintana, 2013 U.S. Dist. LEXIS 12542 (W.D. Pa 2013)("to capture the idea that the incarceration of one whose conduct is not criminal inherently results in a complete miscarriage of justice, most circuits have included an actual innocence component in their savings clause test." id.).

Example of Non-Existent Crime Claim

A good example of a successful non-existent crime claim is found in the case of In Re Davenport, 147 F.3d 605 (7th Cir. 1998).

In Re Davenport was a consolidated appeal involving the cases of two separate petitioners: James Davenport and Sherman Nichols.

Davenport had been convicted as a felon in possession of firearms under 18 U.S.C. § 922(g)(l). He had received an enhanced sentence under Armed Career Criminal Act (18 U.S.C. § 924[e]). His argument was that he was innocent of the Armed Career Criminal Act sentencing enhancement.

Nichols had been convicted of, among other things, the "use" of a firearm in the commission of a drug offense under 18 U.S.C. § 924(c). His argument was that he was actually innocent of the § 924(c) crime in light of the Supreme Court's decision in Bailey v. United States, 516 U.S. 137 (1995) which had redefined and substantially narrowed the element of the § 924(c) crime which prohibits the "use" of a firearm during the commission of a crime of violence or a drug trafficking offense. Specifically, the Bailey court clarified that "use" means "active employment" not just the mere possession of a weapon (such as Nichols had been charged and convicted of).

During this appeal, the Seventh Circuit Court of Appeals found that the main issue with both defendants was whether either of their claims met the definition of actual innocence so that the savings clause contained in 28 U.S.C. § 2255(e) could be applied so that they could file successive habeas petitions.

The Davenport court pointed out that, "Bailey did not change the law under which Nichols was convicted, as in where the Supreme Court overrules one of its previous statutory decisions; Bailey resolved an open question; so mere possessors convicted before Bailey of use really were convicted of a non-existent crime, although this was not widely known at the time." id. at 611.

The Seventh Circuit decided that while Nichols had made a claim that he was convicted of a non-existent crime, Davenport's claim only attacked his sentence, not his underlying conviction. As a result, the Seventh Circuit found that the claim raised by Nichols (non-existent crime) met the definition of actual innocence, while Davenport's claim did not. The court found it necessary to apply the savings clause in § 2255 (e) to Nichols, but denied relief to Davenport. See Davenport at 607-611.

Beware

The Supreme Court in Bousley v. United States, 523 U.S. 614, 624 (1998), made it clear that not only would a movant need to show actual innocence of the charges he was found guilty of, but must also show actual innocence of any charges dropped pursuant to a plea agreement. See e.g. Hampton v. United States, 191 F.3d 695,

703 (6th Cir. 1999); Dejan v. United States, 208 F.3d 682, 686-87 (8th Cir. 2000); and, United States v. Montano, 381 F.3d 1265, 1268-1274 (11th Cir. 2004).

Procedural Default

A petitioner may have his Constitutional claims heard despite procedural default if he can show actual innocence. See e.g. Sawyer v. Whitley, 505 U.S. 333 (1992); and, Murray v. Carrier, 477 U.S. 478, 496 (1986).

AEDPA's Time Bar

Actual innocence, if proved, serves as a gateway through which a petitioner may pass, whether the impediment is a procedural bar or the expiration of the AEDPA time limitations. See e.g. McQuiggin v. Perkins, S.Ct. No. 12-126 (2013).

"Justice is truth in action."

—Benjamin Disraeli, Speech (1851)

II. Miscarriage of Justice

The Supreme Court has recognized a "miscarriage of justice" exception to the interests in finality, comity, and conservation of judicial resources. See e.g. Murray v. Carrier, 477 U.S. 478 (1986)("[I]n appropriate cases...the principles of comity and finality that form the concepts of cause and prejudice must yield to the imperative of correcting a fundamentally unjust incarceration." id. at 495); Kuhlmann v. Wilson, 477 U.S. 436 (1986)(exception to "successive" petitions); McClesky v. Zant, 499 U.S. 467 (1991)(exception to "abusive" petitions); Kenney v. Tamyo-Reyes, 504 U.S. 1 (1992)(exception to failure to develop facts in state court); and, Coleman v. Thompson, 501 U.S. 722 (1991)(exception to procedural rules and filing deadlines).

In Calderon v. Thompson, 523 U.S. 538 (1998), the Supreme Court applied the exception to hold that a federal court may, consistent with the AEDPA, recall its mandate in order to revisit the merits of a decision. id. at 558.

What is a Miscarriage of Justice?

The term "miscarriage of justice" is not an easy one to nail down. The most commonly recognized claim of a miscarriage of justice is when a person is convicted and punished for a non-existent offense or a crime which he did not commit: Actually Innocent. See e.g. Herrera v. Collins, 506 U.S. 390 (1993)("This rule, or fundamental miscarriage of justice exception, is grounded in the 'equitable discretion' of habeas courts to see that federal constitutional errors do not result in the incarceration of innocent persons." id. at 404).

However, there are other situations in which a habeas petitioner might argue that he is a victim of a miscarriage of justice. For example: when a Constitutional error results in the imposition of an unauthorized sentence (See e.g. Wainright v. Sykes, 433 U.S. 72, 91 [1997]); a conviction on a guilty plea tendered solely as a result of faulty advice (see e.g. United States v. Scott, 625 F.2d 623, 625 [5th Cir. 1980]); a lack of factual basis (See e.g. United States v. Gobert, 139 F.3d 436, 438-39 [5th Cir. 1998]); or, an illegal sentence (See e.g. United States v. Paladino, 401 F.3d 471, 483 [7th Cir. 2005]).

It has even been said that "[a]ny wrong result resting on the erroneous application of legal principles is a miscarriage of justice in some degree." Roofing & Sheet Metal Services, Inc. v. La Quinta Motor Inns Inc., 689 F.2d 982, 990 (11th Cir. 1982).

Plain Error Test

In evaluating whether a miscarriage of justice has occurred, a court might apply the "plain error" test. See e.g. Morales-Fernandez v. I.N.S., 418 F.3d 1116 (10th Cir. 2005). "Plain error occurs when there is (1) error, (2) that is plain, which (3) affects substantial rights, and which (4) seriously affects the fairness, integrity, or public reputation of the judicial proceedings." id. at 1122-23.

A good example of plain error would be to permit a defendant to plead guilty to a crime not charged in the indictment. See e.g. United States v. Philips, 869 F.2d 1361, 1364 (10th Cir. 1988)(if an indictment is broadened through amendment other than by the grand jury, amendment constitutes plain error); see also, United States v. Floresca, 38 F.3d 706, 710-12 (4th Cir. 1994)("Convicting a defendant of an unindicted crime affects the fairness, integrity, and public reputation of federal judicial proceedings in a manner most serious." id.).

Example of a Miscarriage of Justice

In Davis v. United States, 417 U.S. 333, 346-47 (1974), the Supreme Court held that when a defendant's conviction and punishment are for "an act that the law does not make criminal," there can be no room for doubt that such circumstances inherently result in a "complete miscarriage of justice."

Procedural Default

The Supreme Court has held there to be an exception to procedural bars in an appropriate case where a petitioner can demonstrate that there has been a miscarriage of justice. See e.g. Bousley v. United States, 523 U.S. 614 at 622 (1998); and, Schlup v. Delo, 513 U.S. 298 at 321 (1995).

AEDPA's Time Bar

The Supreme Court in Day v. McDonough, 547 U.S. 205, 205-10 (2006) decided that a habeas statute of limitations is a type of procedural bar/default and must be treated the same as procedural bars and procedural defaults.

Since the one-year AEDPA time bar must be treated the same as a procedural default (id. McDonough), then it could be argued that, as a procedural default, it cannot be used to bar a petitioner from raising a miscarriage of justice claim because a miscarriage of justice claim cannot be procedurally defaulted. See e.g. Dugger v. Adams, 489 U.S. 401, 414 (1989)("[H]abeas review of a defaulted claim is available, even absent cause for default, if the failure to consider the claim would result in a fundamental miscarriage of justice." id.).

"Laws are like cobwebs, which may catch small flies, but let wasps and hornets break through."

—Jonathan Swift, *A Critical Essay Upon the Faculties of the Mind* (1709)

III. Tolling

Tolling stops the running of a time period, especially the statutory kind such as the Federal Statute of Limitations.

Criminal

Contrary to what many may have thought, the statute of limitations in federal habeas proceeding are not jurisdictional and therefore do not require courts to dismiss claims as soon as the "clock has run." See e.g. Day v. McDonough, 547 U.S. 198, 208 (2006); and, Holland v. Florida, 130 S.Ct. 2549 (2010).

Thus, the statute of limitations in federal habeas proceedings may be tolled.

However, the burden of demonstrating that the AEDPA's one-year limitation should be tolled, whether "equitably" or "statutorily," rest with the petitioner. See e.g. Pace v. DiGuglielmo,

544 U.S. 408, 418 (2005); and, <u>Gaston v. Palmer</u>, 417 F.3d 1030, 1034 (9th Cir. 2005).

Equitable Tolling

In <u>Holland v. Florida</u>, 130 S.Ct. 2549 (2010), the Supreme Court addressed the circumstances in which a federal habeas petitioner could invoke the doctrine of equitable tolling. <u>Holland</u> held that "a habeas petitioner is entitled to equitable tolling only if he shows: (1) that he has been pursuing his rights diligently, and (2) that some extraordinary circumstance stood in his way and prevented timely filing." id.

Due Diligence

The AEDPA does not define the phrase "due diligence," and the phrase has no clearly accepted meaning in the habeas context. See e.g. <u>Johnson v. United States</u>, 544 U.S. 295, 309 n.7 (2007)(AEDPA's due diligence standard is an inexact measure).

To better understand the AEDPA's due diligence standard, see e.g. <u>Moore v. Knight</u>, 368 F.3d 936, 940 (7th Cir. 2004)("a due diligence inquiry should take into account that prisoners are limited by their physical confinement" id.); <u>Aron v. United States</u>, 291 F.3d 708, 711-15 (11th Cir. 2002)("[d]ue diligence...does not require a prisoner to undertake repeated exercises in futility or to exhaust every imaginable option, but rather to make reasonable efforts. Moreover, the due diligence inquiry is an individualized one that must take into account the conditions of confinement and the reality of the prison system"; due diligence determination is "a legal characterization" subject to "clear error review"); and, <u>Ashley v. United States</u>, 266 F.3d 671, 674-75 (7th Cir. 2001)(prisoner's "lack of sophistication could become part of a due diligence analysis because the limitations with which a prisoner is faced might influence how quickly it could have been discovered"; and, district court's assessment of due diligence is reviewed on appeal for "clear error").

The diligence requirement for equitable tolling purposes is "reasonable diligence." See e.g. Lonchar v. Thomas, 517 U.S. 314, 326 (1996); and, Starns v. Andrews, 524 F.3d 612, 618 (5th Cir. 2008).

Extraordinary Circumstances

An example of extraordinary circumstances is when a state or the federal government creates an impediment in violation of the Constitution or laws of the United States prevents a petitioner from timely filing. See e.g. Brady v. Maryland, 373 U.S. 83, 87 (1963)(finding that the withholding of exculpatory evidence that is favorable to the defendant is an unconstitutional impediment).

In some cases, a defendant's own attorney's conduct or actions may meet this standard. See e.g. Holland (attorney's failure to satisfy the professional standards of care); and, United States v. Martin, 408 F.3d 1089, 1096 (8th Cir. 2005) (clients are entitled to equitable tolling when their attorneys retain files, make misleading statements, and engage in poor conduct).

Statutory Tolling

The statutory tolling provisions relevant to a federal habeas petition are found in 28 U.S.C. § 2244(d). These provisions provide tolling of the AEDPA limitations for limited reasons (e.g. retroactive law, newly discovered claims, etc.).

State's Tolling Rules

Ordinarily, a state's tolling rules apply when a state's statute of limitations is borrowed for a federal claim. See e.g. Weis-Buy Servs. Inc. v. Pagilia, 411 F.3d 415, 422 (3rd Cir. 2005).

Since state law governs the applicable statute of limitations in a federal lawsuit (See e.g. Williams v. City of Atlanta, 794 F.2d 624 [11th Cir. 1986]), a plaintiff should look to state law for possible tolling rules and exceptions.

Discovery Rule

The discovery rule tolls a cause of action so that it does not accrue until the injury could have reasonably been discovered. The discovery rule is applied categorically to instances in which the nature of the injury is objectively verifiable. An injury is not inherently undiscoverable when it is the type of injury that could be discovered through the exercise of reasonable diligence. See e.g. Vanderbilt Mortg. & Fin. v. Flores, 692 F.3d 358 (5th Cir. 2012).

Continuing Tort

"Accrual" is when a cause of action becomes enforceable. Generally, accrual occurs when the plaintiff knows or should know that he has suffered the injury that forms the basis of his lawsuit and can identify the person who inflicted the injury. See e.g. Chappell v. Rich, 340 F.3d 1279, 1283 (11th Cir. 2003).

However, it is important to note further that an "allegation of a failure to provide needed and requested medical attention constitutes a continuing tort, which does not accrue until the date medical attention is provided." <u>Lavellee v. Listi</u>, 611 F.2d 1129, 1132 (5th Cir. 1980).

"Time's glory is to calm contending kings, To unmask falsehood and bring truth to light."

—William Shakespeare, *The Rape of Lucrece* (1594)

IV. Fraud On The Court

Fraud on the court has been characterized as "a scheme to interfere with the judicial machinery performing the task of impartial adjudication." <u>Herring v. United States</u>, 424 F.3d 384, 387 n.l (3rd Cir. 2005).

Hazel-Atlas

"Almost all of the principles that govern a claim of fraud on the court find their genesis in <u>Hazel-Atlas Co. v. Hartford-Empire Co.</u>, 322 U.S. 238 (1944) ('Hazel-Atlas'). In <u>Hazel-Atlas</u>, an attorney for Hartford wrote an article praising a Hartford product as an advance in the field, and arranged to have the article printed in a trade journal under the name of an ostensibly disinterested expert. id. at 240. The Patent Office and the Third Circuit relied in part on this article in ruling in favor of Hartford in patent application and infringement cases. id. at 240-41. The Supreme court found conclusive evidence that this article was used for fraudulent purposes, and in granting relief to Hazel-Atlas explained that '[f]rom the beginning there has existed...a rule of equity to the effect that under certain circumstances, one of which is after-discovered fraud, relief will be granted against judgments regardless of the term of their entry.' id. at 244. The court noted further that: 'This is simply not a case of judgment obtained with the aid of a witness who, on the basis of after-discovered evidence, is believed possibly to have been guilty of perjury. Here, even if we consider nothing but Hartford's sworn admissions, we find a deliberately planned and carefully executed scheme to defraud not only the Patent Office, but the Circuit Court of Appeals. Proof of the scheme, and of its complete success up to date, is conclusive.' id. at 245-46." United States v. William, 2012 U.S. Dist. LEXIS 24776 (N.D. Okla. 2012)(quoting Hazel-Atlas).

Criminal and Civil

"The inquiry as to whether a judgment should be set aside for fraud upon the court...focuses not so much in terms of whether the alleged fraud prejudiced the opposing party, but more in terms of whether the alleged fraud harms the integrity of the judicial process." Levander v. Prober, 180 F.3d 114, 1120 (10th Cir. 1999).

In Herring v. United States, 424 F.3d 384 (3rd Cir. 2005), the Third Circuit Court of Appeals stated that "the fraud on the court must constitute 'egregious misconduct'...such as bribery of a judge or fabrication of evidence by counsel." id. at 390, and that "perjury by a witness is not enough to constitute fraud upon the court." id. Thus, a fraud on the court action must satisfy a very demanding standard to justify upsetting the finality of a judgment.

A petitioner must be prepared to make a showing of each of the following prongs: (1) intentional fraud; (2) by an officer of the court;

(3) which is directed at the court itself; (4) in fact deceives the court; and, (5) is supported by clear, unequivocal and convincing evidence. See e.g. <u>Herring</u> at 386-87; and <u>Robinson v. Aktinengesellschaft</u>, 56 F.3d 1259, 1267 (10th Cir. 1995).

Plea Agreements

The Supreme Court has made it clear that the construction and interpretation of plea agreements are matters within the bounds of contract law. See e.g. <u>Ricketts v. Adamson</u>, 483 U.S. 1, 5 n.3 (1987). See also <u>Santobello v. New York</u>, 404 U.S. 257, 262-263 (1971)(plea agreements are "contracts").

If a party commits fraud while negotiating a contract, the contract is void as if it never existed. See e.g. <u>Godly v. United States</u>, 5 F.3d 1473, 1476 (Fed, Cir. 1993)("A contract tainted by fraud...is void ab intio").

Vehicle to Present the Claim

"Rule 60" of the Federal Rules of Civil Procedure contemplates two avenues for relief from fraud on the court: an independent action for relief from an order; or, a motion of invoking the inherent power of a court to set aside its judgment if procured by fraud. See e.g. <u>United States v. Buck</u>, 281 F.3d 1336, 1341 (10th Cir. 2002).

Independent Action

An independent action under Rule 60(d)(1) is "an independent action in equity to obtain relief from a judgment." <u>Mitchell v. Rees</u>, 651 F.3d 593, 595 (6th Cir. 20ll)(quoting: 11 C. Wright & A. Miller, Federal Practice & Procedure § 2868, at 237-38 [1973]).

The elements of an independent action are: (1) a judgment which should not, in equity and good conscience be enforced; (2) a good defense to the alleged cause of action for which the judgment is founded; (3) fraud, accident, or mistake which prevented the defendant in the judgment from obtaining the benefit of his defense; (4) the absence of fault or negligence on part of the defendant; and (5) the absence of any adequate remedy at law. See e.g. Barrett v. Sec'y of Health & Human Svcs, 840 F.2d 1259, 1263 (6th Cir. 1987).

Invoking the Court's Inherent Power

All courts have the inherent equitable power to vacate a judgment that has been obtained through the commission of fraud upon the court. See e.g. Universal Oil Prods. Co. v. Root Ref. Co., 328 U.S. 575, 580 (1946).

Rule 60(d)(3)allows a court to relieve a party of judgment upon the showing of fraud, misrepresentation, or other misconduct of an adverse party, "however, because of their very potency, inherent powers, must be exercised with restraint and discretion." Chambers v. NASCO, Inc., 501 U.S. 32, 44 (1991).

Moreover, not only does a court possess the inherent authority to consider such fraud, the court "has a duty to consider whether there has been a fraud on the court, and if so, to order an appropriate remedy, whenever such fraud comes to the court's attention." In Re M.T.G. Inc., 366 B.R. 730, 754 (E.D. Mich. 2007).

Further, "the inherent power of a court to set aside its judgment if procured by fraud upon the court is not dependent on the filing of a motion by a party: the court may assert this power sua sponte." United States v. Buck, 281 F.3d 1336, 1342 (10th Cir. 2002).

AEDPA's Time Bar

Typically, motions to set aside judgments are subject to a one-year time bar. See Fed.R. iv.P. 60(b)(3). If, however, a person alleges that fraud was committed against the court, there is no such bar. Fed.R.Civ.P. 60(c)(I).

Fed.R.Civ.P. 60(d)(3) states: "This rule does not limit a court's power to...set aside a judgment for fraud on the court." Rule 60(d)(3) thus allows a claimant to escape any time bars set into place. See e.g. <u>Parkhurst v. Pittsburgh Paints Inc.</u>, 399 Fedd. Appx. 341, (10th Cir. 2005); and, <u>Zurich N. Am. v. Matrix Serv.</u>, 426 F.3d 1281, 1291 (10th Cir. 2005). As one circuit court has explained, "a decision produced by fraud on the court is not in essence a decision at all and never becomes final." <u>Kenner v. Comm'r of International Revenue</u>, 387 F.2d 689, 691 (7th Cir. 1968).

Criminal

Notably, when a habeas petitioner files a motion for relief from a judgment based on a fraud on the court, it will not be considered as a second or successive habeas motion. See e.g. <u>Burke v. United States</u>, 2005 U.S. Dist. LEXIS 25908, (E.D. Pa. 2005); <u>Calderon v. Thompson</u>, 523 U.S. 532, 553 (1998); <u>United States v. McVeigh</u>, 9 Fed. Appx. 980 (10th Cir. 200l)(noting fraud on the court exception to the gatekeeping requirements and affirmative limitations in § 2255 applicable to successive motions); <u>Workman v. Bell</u>, 227 F.3d 331, 335 (6th Cir. 2000)(recognizing exception); and <u>United States v. Williams</u>, 2012 U.S. Dist. LEXIS 24776 (N.D. Okla. 2012)(same).

Example of Fraud on the Court Claim

In United States v. Williams, 2012 U.S. Dist. LEXIS 24776 (N.D. Okla 2012), the criminal defendant moved the court to "Withdraw and Nullify Guilty Plea" in light of new evidence that demonstrated the judgment was the product of fraud upon the court. The court found that the newly asserted allegations were more properly and liberally construed as a motion asserted pursuant to Fed.R.Civ.P. 60(d)(3). Specifically, the defendant alleged that the federal prosecutor, and/or its agents, fabricated evidence and used perjured testimony to procure the search warrants, indictment, and superseding indictments in the case. These documents were relied upon by the court in both the acceptance of the defendant's guilty plea, as well as in sentencing. As a result, the court found that the defendant's definitive and precise accusations met the requirement that a defendant must allege that it was an officer of the court who presented fabricated evidence (See e.g. Herring v. United States, 424 F.3d 384 [3rd Cir. 2005]).

Beware

Some courts has expressed an opinion that they may not have the inherent power in a criminal case to set aside a void judgment pursuant to a fraud on the court claim. See e.g. Unites States v. Brown, 2013 U.S. Dist. LEXIS 99616 (E.D. Pa. 2013)("while an 'inherent power' in equity to set aside civil judgments has long been recognized, the propriety of such an act in the criminal context is questionable").

It is my belief that a criminal court has more power than a civil court because it deals in matters of life and liberty rather than mere monetary matters. Therefore it is very hard to believe that a civil defendant is afforded more protection under the law than that of a criminal defendant.

If you have a fraud on the court claim in your criminal case and your court tries to say that it does not have the inherent power to set aside the void judgment, you should not give up, but take the matter all the way to the Supreme Court, if necessary. But not all courts have taken this illogical position, so make sure you do thorough research on this point.

"Laws grind the poor, and rich men rule the law."

—Oliver Goldsmith, *The Traveller* (1764)

V. Retroactive Law

The Supreme Court, in <u>Teague v. Lane</u>, 489 U.S. 288 (1989) made it so that, in general, a petitioner cannot raise habeas claims based on new rule of law. This is known as the "Teague Rule."

However, there are exceptions to the "Teague Rule" that allow you to use new rule of law.

Definition of New Law

The Supreme Court has stated that "it is admittedly often difficult to determine when a [Supreme Court] case announces a new rule." <u>Penry v. Linaugh</u>, 492 U.S. 302 (1989). A "new rule" is one that breaks new ground or imposes a new obligation on the government, and is not dictated by precedent existing at the time a conviction becomes final. id. See also <u>Butler v. McKellar</u>, 494 U.S. 407, 415 (1990)(Courts frequently view their decisions as being controlled by previous precedent).

Procedural vs. Substantive

New rules of law are either "procedural" or "substantive. " Sometimes a decision can be made up of both, but not typically.

A new rule is "procedural" if it regulates the manner of determining a defendant's culpability. See e.g. Schriro v. Summerlin, 542 U.S. 348, 352-353 (2004).

A new rule is "substantive" if it alters the range of conduct or the class of persons the law can punish. See e.g. Schriro v. Summerlin, 542 U.S. 348, 352-353 (2004).

Retroactivity

A new "procedural" rule of law is not retroactive unless it is a "watershed" rule. Schriro, 542 U.S. at 352.

"Watershed" rules dictate criminal procedures, ensuring the fairness and accuracy of a criminal proceeding. See e.g. Saffle v. Parks, 494 U.S. 484, 495 (1990). In order to qualify as "watershed," a rule must: (1) alter the understanding of the bedrock procedural elements essential to the fairness of the proceeding, and (2) announce a new rule without which an accurate conviction is diminished. See e.g. Whorton v. Brockting, 549 U.S. 406, 418 (2007). It is not likely that a new "procedural" rule will meet these requirements since "this class of rules is extremely narrow." Schiriro, 542 U.S. at 352.

A new "substantive" rule, on the other hand, is always retroactive. Schiriro at 351.

Three Types of New Law to Look For

There are three types of new law that you should look for:

1. new laws prohibiting certain types of punishment, and

2. new laws decriminalizing certain behavior (both which the Supreme Court must explicitly state are retroactive); and

3. the Supreme Court's decisions construing substantive federal criminal statutes (which are automatically given retroactive treatment).

1. Prohibited Punishments

An example of a new rule of law prohibiting a certain type of punishment is found in Roper v. Simmons, 543 U.S. 551, 568 (2005). In Roper the Supreme Court held that prisoners who were under eighteen years old when their crimes were committed must not receive the death penalty.

2. Decriminalized Behavior

An example of a new rule of law that decriminalized certain behavior is found in Griswold v. Connecticut, 381 U.S. 479, 485-86 (1965). In Griswold the Supreme Court held that the Connecticut law against using contraception violated the Constitutional right to marital privacy.

3. Decisions Construing Substantive Federal Criminal Statutes

"[Teague] is inapplicable to the situation in which the court decides the meaning of a criminal statute enacted by Congress." Bousley v. United States, 523 U.S. 614 (1998). See also Schiriro v. Summerlin, 542 U.S. 348, 354 (2004) ("New substantive rules generally apply retroactively. This includes decisions that narrow the scope of a criminal statute by interpreting its terms."); and, Gonzales v.

Crosby, 545 U.S. 524 (2005)("A change in the interpretation of a substantive statute may have consequences for cases that have already reached final judgment, particularly in the criminal context.").

A successful example of where a petitioner raised a Supreme Court decision construing a substantive federal criminal statute is found in the case of United States v. Peter, 310 F.3d 709 (11th Cir. 2002): In 1996 Peter pled guilty to a superseding information that charged him with a single count of conspiring to violate the Racketeering Influenced and Corrupt Organizations Act ("RICO"). A plea agreement filed by the parties explicitly stated that the only predicate crime supporting the RICO conspiracy was mail fraud under 18 U.S.C. § 1341 based on Peter's admission to including misrepresentations in license applications he mailed to the Florida Division of Alcoholic Beverages and Tobacco. As a result, Peter was given a $25,000 fine and was sentenced to 24 months in prison to be followed by two years of supervised release. Having pled guilty, Peter did not directly appeal his sentence of imprisonment and was released on May 6, 1998. Peter's period of supervised release ended on May 5, 2000.

On November 7, 2000, the Supreme Court decided Clevand v. United States, 531 U.S. 12 (2000). Roughly a year later, Peter filed a challenge to his RICO conviction by way of a petition for "Writ of Error Coram Nobis," arguing that the Supreme Court's decision in Clevand has established that the act forming the basis for his guilty plea did not constitute the predicated crime of mail fraud. The government never responded to the petition. On November 27, 2002, without a hearing, the district court entered a summary order denying him any relief. Peter filed a timely notice of appeal from that order. The Eleventh Circuit Court of Appeals sided with Peter and the judgment of the district court was reversed and the case was remanded because the district court had abused its discretion in summarily dismissing the petition because a "Writ of Error Coram Nobis" was indeed necessary to correct the original criminal judgment. As the Court of Appeals noted, decisions of the Supreme Court construing federal criminal statutes must be given retroactive effect. See also, Bousley v. United States, 523 U.S. 614 (1998).

Applicability of New Rules of Law

New rules apply to all cases that are still on direct appeal. See e.g. Griffith v. Kentucky, 479 U.S. 314, 322-323 (1987). While only retroactive new rules apply to cases that have already become final. See, e.g. Chaidez v. United States, 133 S.Ct. 1103, 1107 (2013).

"It is better that ten guilty persons escape than one innocent suffer."

—William Blackstone, *Commentaries on the Laws of England (1765)*

VI. Newly Discovered Evidence

Criminal

The AEDPA has imposed a one year period of limitation for filing a motion to vacate, set aside, or correct a sentence. See e.g. 28 U.S.C. § 2255. However, the AEDPA allows petitioners to file within one year of the discovery of new evidence, or facts supporting the claim or claims. See e.g. 28 U.S.C. § 2255 (f).

Due Diligence

It is important to note though, that the AEDPA requires a showing that the new evidence or facts supporting the claim or claims could not have been discovered earlier. This requires a petitioner to show that he has exercised "due diligence" in the discovery of this new evidence or facts. If a court finds that a petitioner exercised due diligence, then the one year limitation period would begin to run on the date the petitioner actually discovered the relevant facts.

Notably, the AEDPA does not require the maximum feasible diligence, but only "due" or "reasonable" diligence. See e.g. Wims v. United States, 225 F.3d 186, 190 n.4 (2nd Cir. 2000). "Due diligence therefore does not require a prisoner to undertake repeated exercises in futility or to exhaust every imaginable option, but rather to make reasonable efforts. Moreover, the due diligence inquiry is an individual one that must take into account the conditions of confinement and the reality of the prison system." Aron v. United States, 291 F.3d 708 (11th Cir. 2002); see also Easterwood v. Champion, 213 F.3d 1321, 1323 (10th Cir. 2000).

Actual Innocence

When the new evidence is the kind that meets the definition of "actual innocence," the AEDPA time bar, all procedural bars, and the "due diligence" inquiry is overcome. See e.g. McQuiggin v. Perkins, S.Ct. No. 12-126 (2013).

Civil

Generally, a motion for a new civil trial must be filed with the clerk no later than 28 days after the entry of judgment. See e.g. Fed.R.Civ.P. 59(b); and, Fed.R.Civ.P. 50(b). The deadline for filing a motion for a new trial is jurisdictional and cannot be extended by the court or parties. However, Fed.R.Civ.P. 60(b) allows the parties to seek relief from the judgment, that is, to motion the court to set aside the judgment for many reasons, including newly discovered evidence.

VI. Newly Discovered Evidence

The time to file a motion for relief from the judgment under Rule 60(b) in light of newly discovered evidence must be filed within one year after the judgment or order is entered. Fed.R.Civ.P. 60(b) (2).

It is important to note though that motions under Rule 60(b) (2) on the grounds of newly discovered evidence are usually viewed with disfavor and require the movant to satisfy four prongs. See e.g. U.S. X'press Enters v. J.B. Hunt Transp., 320 F.3d 809 (8th Cir. 2003). "In order to prevail under Rule 60(b)(2), the movant must show that (1) the evidence was discovered after trial; (2) due diligence was exercised to discover the evidence; (3) the evidence is material and not merely cumulative or impeaching; and (4) the evidence is such that a new trial would probably produce a different result." id. at 815.

"The truth which makes men free is for the most part the truth which men prefer not to hear."

—Herbert Agar, *A Time for Greatness* (1942)

VII. Jurisdiction

All federal courts are courts of limited jurisdiction deriving their power solely from Article III of the Constitution and legislative acts of Congress. See e.g. <u>Insurance Corp. of Ireland. Ltd. v. Compagnie des Bauxites de Guinee</u>, 456 U.S. 694, 701 (1982). The courts therefore cannot derive power to act from the actions or inactions of the parties before them. (<u>Insurance Corp. of Ireland. Ltd.</u> at 702). Consequently, the parties are incapable of conferring upon the courts a jurisdictional foundation they otherwise lack simply by waiver or procedural default. See e.g. <u>United States v. Griffin</u>, 302 U.S. 226, 229 (1938).

Criminal

There are more than a few different types of jurisdiction (i.e. Personal, Territorial, Subject-matter, etc.), but the one most relevant to post-conviction relief in a criminal matter is that of "Subject-matter Jurisdiction."

Subject-matter Jurisdiction

Subject-matter Jurisdiction ("SMJ" hereafter) defines a court's authority to hear and decide a certain type of claim. See e.g. United States v. Morton, 467 U.S. 822, 828 (1984).

You see, Congress's grant of jurisdiction in criminal cases only extends to offenses against the United States. See 28 U.S.C. § 3231. This is why any error in SMJ implicates a court's power to adjudicate the matter before it.

See e.g. Louisville & Nashville Railroad Co. v. Mottley, 211 U.S. 149, 152 (1908). A court will even raise lack of SMJ on its own. (Insurance Corp. of Ireland. Ltd. at 702).

Void Not Merely Voidable

"The Supreme Court has summarized the effect of judgments rendered without jurisdiction: Courts are constituted by authority and they cannot go beyond the power delegated to them. If they act beyond that authority, and certainly in contravention of it, their judgments and orders are regarded as nullities. They are not voidable but simply void, and this even prior to reversal." Burleson v. Coastal Recreation Inc., 595 F.2d 332, 337 (5th Cir. 1978)(citations omitted).

"A jurisdictional defect is one that strip[s] the court of its power to act and makes its judgment void." United States v. McCoy, 266 F.3d 1245, 1249 (11th Cir. 2001).

"A void act is neither a law or command. It is a nullity. It confers no authority." Hopkins v. Clemson, 221 U.S. 636, 644 (1911).

"Jurisdictional error is by its nature of such a 'fundamental character' as to render proceedings 'irregular and invalid.' When a court without jurisdiction convicts and sentences a defendant, the conviction and sentence are 'void from their inception and remain void long after a defendant has fully suffered their direct force.' " United States v. Peter, 310 F.3d 709 (11th Cir. 2002)(quoting: United States v. Morgan, 346 U.S. 502 at 509 [1954]; and, Spencer v. Kemna, 523 U.S. 1 at 43 [1998]).

Examples of Jurisdictional Errors

A jurisdictional error was successfully raised in the case Harris v. United States, 149 F.3d 1304 (11th Cir. 1998). In Harris, the government failed to file an Information to establish the defendant's prior conviction before he entered his guilty plea as required by 21 U.S.C. § 85l(a)(l). Because the government failed to do this before the acceptance of the guilty plea, the district court plainly lacked jurisdiction to impose the enhanced sentence. Accordingly, the defendant's sentence was reversed for resentencing.

One of the most relevant criminal cases concerning jurisdictional defects is United States v. Meacham, 626 F.2d 503 (5th Cir. 1980). In Meacham the former Fifth Circuit of Appeals reversed the convictions of five defendants who had been charged with "conspiring to attempt" to import marijuana with the intent to distribute it. id. at 507. The court found that Congress had not intended for the statute which the government relied to create "the conceptually bizarre crime of conspiracy to attempt." id. at 508-09.

Indictments

A claim is said to be jurisdictional if it can be resolved by examining the face of the indictment or the record at the time of the plea without requiring further proceedings. See e.g. United States v. Caperell, 938 F.2d 975, 977-78 (9th Cir. 1991).

An indictment's relationship to jurisdiction is based on whether it alleges conduct constituting a federal offense. If an indictment fails to charge such an offense, then a court has no basis for exercising jurisdiction. See e.g. United States v. McIntosh, 704 F.3d 894, (11th Cir. 2013). Therefore, an indictment suffers from a "jurisdictional defect" when it charges no crime at all, or rather when the government alleges a specific course of conduct outside the reach of the applicable statute. See e.g. Mayberry v. United States, 156. Fed. Appx. 265 (11th Cir. 2005).

No Indictment

"Unless there is a valid waiver, the lack of an indictment in a federal felony case is a defect going to the jurisdiction of the court." United States v. Montgomery, 628 F.2d 414 (5th Cir. 1980).

Not All Claims Are Jurisdictional

One of the many failed jurisdictional arguments is found in McCoy v. United States, 266 F.3d 1245 (11th Cir. 2001). In McCoy, the petitioner argued that his sentence was illegal under Apprendi v. New Jersey, 530 U.S. 466 (2000). Specifically, McCoy contended that the indictment, because it did not allege a specific drug quantity, violated the Fifth Amendment's indictment clause, thus depriving the court of jurisdiction to sentence him under 21 U.S.C. § 84l(b)(l)(A). The court concluded however that a claim of Apprendi error is not jurisdictional.

In McCoy, the Eleventh Circuit Court of Appeals went on to distinguish the type of indictment problems involved in Meacham, where "the indictment is defective because it charged no crime at all," from indictment defects that do not give rise to jurisdictional error; such as the one raised by McCoy. id. at 1253-54. Similarly, in United States v. Sanchez, 269 F.3d 1250 (11th Cir. 2001) (en banc), the court distinguished between the claim that a defendant had been charged under a preempted statute and the claim that an indictment failed to charge an element of the offense. (Sanchez at 1275 n.48). As the Sanchez court had recognized the, the preempted statute claim was held to be of jurisdictional dimension in the case United States v. Tomeny, 144 F.3d 749 (11th Cir. 1998). By describing Tomeny as "inapposite," Sanchez reaffirmed the importance of the distinction between indictment omissions and the affirmative allegation of a specific course of conduct that is not proscribed by the charging statute.

Another non-jurisdictional argument is found in Mayberry v. United States, Fed. Appx. 265 (11th Cir. 2005). In Mayberry, the defendant incorrectly asserted that count two of his indictment suffered from a jurisdictional defect because it charged multiple financial transactions as a criminal money laundering offense under 18 U.S.C. § 1956 (a)(l)(i), the court found instead that the defendant's argument was actually a duplicity argument which is not a true jurisdictional claim.

Raised Anytime

In Gonzales v. Crosby, 545 U.S. 524 (2005), the Supreme Court made it clear that the age-old civil law principles apply to habeas corpus cases, in particular, opportunities to obtain vacator of a judgment that is void for lack of SMJ, no matter the passage of time. This being consistent with the precept that: defects in subject-matter jurisdiction may be raised at anytime. See e.g. City of Kenosha v. Bruno, 412 U.S. 507 (1973); and, Philbrook v. Glodgett, 421 U.S. 707 (1975).

Civil law tells us that a judgment that is void at its inception remains as such. See e.g. United States v. One Toshiba Color Television, 213 F.3d 147, (3rd Cir. 2000): "[T]here are no time limits with regards to a challenge to a void judgment because of its status of a nullity..."; "[N]o passage of time can render a void judgment valid..." id.

"[A] void judgment is one so affected by a fundamental infirmity that the infirmity may be raised even after the judgment becomes final..." United Student Aid Funds, Inc. v. Espinosa, 559 U.S. 260, 270 (2010).

Procedural Default

A defendant can procedurally default many of his Constitutional rights. (See e.g. Levine v. United States, 362 U.S. 610, 619-20 [1960][Sixth Amendment right to be confronted with one's accusers]; United States v. Brasco, 742 F.2d 1335, 1365 [11th Cir. 1984][Fifth Amendment protection from double jeopardy]; etc.). Then upon collateral attack, he must show "cause and prejudice" to justify his failure to timely assert his Constitutional rights, (See e.g. Coulter v. Herring, 60 F.3d 1499 [11th Cir. 1995]), or his failure to assert his claim on direct appeal (See e.g. United States v. Frady, 456 U.S. 152 [1982]). In fact, the Supreme Court has admonished that "if the defendant had counsel and was tried by an impartial adjudicator, there is a strong presumption that any other Constitutional errors are subject to harmless-error analysis." Rose v. Clark, 478 U.S. 570, 579 (1986). However, "jurisdictional" claims, by contrast, cannot be procedurally defaulted, nor are they subject to harmless error analysis (See e.g. McCoy v. United States, 266 F.3d 1245 [11th Cir. 2001]); nor must a defendant show "cause and prejudice" to raise such a claim (See e.g. Harris v: United States, 149 F.3d 1304, 1309 [11th Cir. 1998]).

AEDPA's Time Bar

A void judgment is a legal nullity and a court considering to vacate has no discretion in determining whether it should be set aside. See e.g. 7 J. Moore, Federal Practice. 60. 25 [2] (2nd Ed. 1973); Recreational Props. Inc. Southwest Mortg. Serv. Corp., 804 F.2d 311, 313-14 (5th Cir. 1986); and, Jordan v. Gilligan, 500 F.2d 701, 704 (6th Cir. 1974); United States v. Bethancourth, 554 F.3d 132g, 2009 WL 66420 at *3 (11th Cir. 2009)(the court has an independent obligation, regardless of the stage of the proceedings and independent of a specific timely request from the parties, to correct defects in subject-matter jurisdiction).

The only question here is whether the AEDPA's time bar will excuse a court from its obligation to inquire into its excess in SMJ. Or, to put it in a simpler format: is jurisdictional error an exception to the AEDPA's one year time bar?

As the Supreme Court has noted, "Subject-matter jurisdiction is an Art. III as well as a statutory requirement; it functions as a restriction on federal power, and contributes to the characterization of the federal sovereign. Certain legal consequences directly follow from this. For example, no action of the parties can confer subject-matter jurisdiction upon a federal court. Thus, the consent of the parties is irrelevant, principles of estoppel do not apply, and a party does not waive the requirement by failing to challenge jurisdiction early in the proceedings." id. Insurance Corp. of Ireland. Ltd. v. Compagnie des Bauxites de Guinee, 456 U.S. 694, at 705 (1982).

A void conviction "can not be the cause of imprisonment – not withstanding any procedural default." Gonzales v. Abbott, 967 F.2d 1499 (11th Cir. 1992).

The Supreme Court itself, in <u>Day v. McDonough</u>, 547 U.S. 205, 210 (2006) recognized that a habeas statute of limitations is a type of procedural bar/default: "AEDPA's statute of limitations advance the same concerns as those advanced by the doctrines of exhaustion and procedural default, and must be treated the same." id.

The Supreme Court decided a few years later in <u>Holland v. Florida</u>, 177 L.Ed 2d 130 (2010) that the AEDPA statute of limitations is not jurisdictional and the time limitation is thus subject to waiver and forfeiture. id.

Since the AEDPA time bar must be treated the same as a procedural default (id. <u>McDonough</u>), then logic tells us that, as a procedural default, it cannot be used to bar a petitioner from raising a jurisdictional error because jurisdictional error cannot be procedurally defaulted (See e.g. <u>United States v. Griffin</u>, 303 U.S. 226, 229 [1938]; <u>Harris v. United States</u>, 149 F.3d 1304, 1308-09 [11th Cir. 1998]; and, <u>United States v. Peter</u>, 310 F.3d 709, 712 [11th Cir. 2002]). For instance, the Supreme Court in <u>Young v. United States</u>, 535 U.S. 43, 49 (2002), stated that it is hornbook law that limitation periods are "customarily subject to equitable tolling." id. This, in conjunction with the fact that the AEDPA is no more than a non-jurisdictional affirmative defense (id. <u>McDonough</u>), tells us that the AEDPA time bar is no more than a type of "laches":

> **laches.** 1. Unreasonable delay in pursuing a right
> or claim--almost always an equitable one--in a way
> that prejudices the party against whom relief is
> sought. 2. The equitable doctrine by which a court
> denies relief to a claimant who has unreasonably
> delayed in asserting the claim, when that delay
> has prejudiced the party against whom relief is
> sought. id.
> —Black's Law Dict. (7th Ed.)

As discussed previously, a judgment entered without jurisdiction is void (See e.g. <u>Burnham v. Superior Court of California, County of Marin</u>, 110 S.Ct. 2105 (1990). And nowhere in the law is it logical to allow an affirmative defense such as "laches" operate as a bar to vacate a void judgment. See e.g. <u>Kao Hwa Shipping Co. v. China Steel Corp.</u>, 816 F.Supp. 910, 913 (S. Dist. N.Y. 1993)(laches do not apply to a void judgment); <u>Crosby v. Bradstreet Co.</u>, 312 F.2d 483 (2nd Cir. 1962) (vacating a void judgment 30 years after entry), cert. denied, 373 U.S. 911 (1963); <u>Taft v. Donellan Jerome, Inc.</u>, 407 F.2d 807, 808 (7th Cir. 1969)(allowing challenge to jurisdiction 13 years after final judgment); <u>Austin v. Smith</u>, 114 U.S. App. D.C. 97, 312 F.2d 337, 343 (D.C. Cir. 1962)(laches never apply to a void judgment); <u>Battle Liberty Nat'l Life Ins. Co.</u>, 974 F.2d 1279 (11th Cir. 1992)(per curiam), aff'g, 770 F.Supp. 1499, 1511-12 (M.D. Ala. 1991)(laches are inapplicable), cert. denied, _U.S._, 133 S.Ct. 2999 (1993); and, <u>In Re Center Wholesale</u>, 759 F.2d 1440, 1447 (9th Cir. 1985)("[A] void judgment cannot acquire validity because of laches.").

"LACHES" is an affirmative defense. See, Fed.R.Civ.P. 8(c)(1).

"WAIVER" is an affirmative defense. See, Fed.R.Civ.P. 8(c)(1).

"ESTOPPEL" is an affirmative defense. See, Fed.R.Civ.P 8(c)(1).

"PROCEDURAL DEFAULT" is an: affirmative defense. See, e.g. <u>Gray v. Netherland</u>, 518 U.S. 152, 165-66 (1996).

"AEDPA's STATUTE OF LIMITATIONS" is an affirmative defense. See, e.g. <u>Day v. McDonough</u>, 547 U.S. 198, 205, 210 n.11 (2006).

From a logical standpoint, it would be clearly unsound to uphold a void conviction due to a defect in subject-matter jurisdiction in light of the AEDPA's non-jurisdictional "statute of limitations" which itself is just another affirmative defense like "laches," "procedural default," and "waiver." The Supreme Court pretty much spelled this out in Day v. McDonough, when it said "AEDPA's statute of limitations advances the same concerns as those advanced by the doctrines of exhaustion and procedural default, and must be treated the same." id. 537 U.S. 198, 204-10 (2006).

Thus, to time bar a claim raising a defect in subject-matter jurisdiction is, essentially, to treat the AEDPA's statute of limitations different than the doctrines of exhaustion and procedural default, which is inconsistent with both law and logic.

Beware

I saved jurisdiction for last because it is the most controversial out of the seven ways to overcome the federal statute of limitations.

Courts simply do not like to be told that they do not have jurisdiction over a certain type of case or claim. In order to maintain power (jurisdiction) over individuals, courts will grasp at any straw to help keep afloat their sinking position, even though it may be beyond logic or law.

There is an ongoing problem with federal courts time barring claims of jurisdictional error. And this problem will not be resolved until the US Supreme Court steps in to correct the problem.

From what I have seen, Barreto-Barreto v. United States, 551 F.3d 95 (1st Cir. 2008) is the go-to case for many district and circuit courts to argue and decide that the AEDPA's statute of limitations bars all "jurisdictional" claims outside of its one-year time limit.

In Barreto-Barreto, the petitioners asserted that the sentencing court did not have subject-matter jurisdiction because the informations to which they pled guilty did not actually charge a crime and that their jurisdictional challenge is not subject to the AEDPA's time bar.

The First Circuit Court of Appeals rejected the petitioner's argument in Barreto-Barreto stating that § 2255 states that claims which allege "the court was without jurisdiction to impose such sentence" may be raised in a § 2255 motion seeking to vacate the sentence and that "[a] 1-year period of limitation shall apply to a motion under this section." 28 U.S.C. § 2255 (a), (f), and nothing in the language of § 2255 suggests that jurisdictional challenges are exempt from the one-year limitations period, to the contrary, § 2255 (f) explicitly states that the limitations period "shall apply" to all motions under § 2255. id. Barreto-Barreto at 100.

Many circuits have followed suit on this issue and cite Barreto-Barreto to deny petitioners relief. See e.g. United States v. Card, 534 Fed. App'x 765 (10th Cir. 2013)(denying COA and rejecting petitioner's argument that jurisdictional challenge was not subject to § 2255's limitation period); United States v. Scruggs, 691 F.3d 660, 667 (5th Cir. 2012)(movant was not excused from including claim in his § 2255 motion because "the statutory limitations on § 2255 review apply to jurisdictional claims"); Williams v. United States, 383 Fed. App'x 927 (11th Cir. 2010)(following Barreto-Barreto and holding that § 2255's 1-year limit "applies even though [petitioner's] new claim is an attack on the district court's jurisdiction).

However, Barreto-Barreto is not very persuasive when you look deeper into the issue:

While the claim of a court being "without jurisdiction to impose such sentence" is indeed specifically listed as a ground for § 2255 relief, that pertinent phrase: "the court was without jurisdiction to impose such **sentence**" (id. at § 2255[a])(emphasis added) does not encompass all "types" of jurisdiction, namely "subject-matter jurisdiction," the court's authority to hear and decide a certain type of **claim.** See e.g. United States v. Morton, 467 U.S. 822, 828 (1984)(emphasis added).

A defect in subject-matter jurisdiction is one that "strips the court of its **power to act** and makes its **judgment** void." Escareno v. Carl Nolte Sohne GmbH & Co., 77 F.3d 407, 412 (11th Cir. 1996)(emphasis added).

Section 2255 does not itself address the issue of a **void judgment** due to an excess in subject-matter jurisdiction. It only addresses the issue of an improper **sentence** based on the erroneous exercise of judgment which is in fact distinguishable. See e.g. McCoy v. United States, 266 F.3d 1245, 1253-54 (11th Cir. 2001); United States v. Sanchez, 269 F.3d 1250 (11th Cir. 200l)(en banc); and, United States v. Peter, 310 F.3d 709, 714-15 (11th Cir. 2002); Lubben v. Selective Serv. Syst. 453 F.2d 645, 649 (1st Cir. 1972); and, Schlesinger v. Councilman, 420 U.S. 738, 746 (1975)(same).

Also, it is worth noting that Barreto-Barreto was decided in 2008, two years before the Supreme Court make it clear in Holland v. Florida, 177 L.Ed 2d 130 (2010) that the AEDPA statute of limitations is not jurisdictional and the time limit is thus subject to waiver and forfeiture. Barreto-Barreto is thus obviously inconsistent with Holland v. Florida because it effectively treats the AEDPA statute of limitations like it is jurisdictional.

Therefore, for the above-stated reasons, this issue is ripe for challenge and the United States Supreme Court is the appropriate venue to raise this challenge. In my view, for the above-stated reasons, Barreto-Barreto and other cases like it are wrong and the Supreme Court needs to step in and make it clear to these district and circuit courts that the AEDPA's statute of limitation s is not something that can be used to ignore a defect in a court's subject-matter jurisdiction.

Vehicle to Present the Claim

The law recognizes that there must be a vehicle to correct errors "of the most fundamental character; that is, such as rendered the proceeding itself irregular and invalid." United States v. Morgan, 346 U.S. 502, at 509 n.15 (1954).

One type of claim that has historically been recognized as fundamental, and for which collateral relief has been available accordingly, is that of jurisdictional dimension. See e.g. United States v. Addonizio, 442 U.S. 178 (1979).

Courts are bound to assure themselves of jurisdiction even if the parties fail to raise the issue. A court will raise lack of SMJ "Sua Sponte." See e.g. Insurance Corp. of Ireland. Ltd., at 702.

If the defendant is still incarcerated and the court has not raised the issue, the defendant might try to raise the issue himself by way of a "motion to vacate" (e.g. § 2255 motion) in the court which convicted him. For a federal defendant in federal custody this would likely be pursuant to 28 U.S.C. § 2255. See e.g. United States v. Harper, 901 F.2d 471, 472 (5th Cir. 1990); and, Harris v. United States, (11th Cir. 1998). Or, if § 2255 is not available, the defendant could try to raise the issue himself by a petition to the court located in the district where he is incarcerated for "Habeas Corpus" relief pursuant to 28 U.S.C. § 2241. See e.g. United States v. Addonizio, 442 U.S. 178, 185. (1979) (Habeas Corpus has long been available to attack convictions and sentences entered by a court without jurisdiction).

For a defendant who has already used his § 2255 motion (or 28 U.S.C. § 2254 motion for a state prisoner) in a previous attack on other grounds, a motion under "Rule 60(b)" of the Federal Rules of Civil Procedure may be a viable tool to challenge the court's SMJ. See e.g. United States v. Landry, 2006 U.S. Dist. LEXIS 7226 (M.D.

Fla. 2006). Notably, in Hertz Corp. v. Alamo Rent-A-Car Inc., 16 F.3d 1126, 1130-31 (11th Cir. 1994), the Eleventh Circuit Court of Appeals concluded that Rule 60(b)(4) is not subject to the Rule 60's reasonable time limitation. However, be advised, the Supreme Court in Gonzales v. Crosby, 545 U.S. 524 (2005) held that a proper Rule 60(b) motion "attacks not the substance of a federal court's resolution on the merits, but some defect in the integrity of the federal habeas corpus proceedings."

If none of these options prove to be available a defendant may request that the court that convicted him issue a "Writ of Audita Querela" under the All Writs Act. See e.g. 28 U.S.C. § 1651. As the Supreme Court has noted an "extraordinary remedy" is available "only under the circumstances compelling such action to achieve justice," to right "errors of the most fundamental character." United States v. Morgan, 346 U.S. 502 at 511 n.15. As noted before, jurisdictional errors are "fundamental." See e.g. United States v. Addonizio, 442 U.S. 178 (1979); and Moody v. United States, 847 F.2d 1575, 1576-77 (11th Cir. 1989).

No Longer Incarcerated

If a defendant is no longer incarcerated, he might try to raise the issue himself by way of a petition to the court of his conviction for the issuance of a "Writ of Error Coram Nobis" under the All Writs Act. See e.g.28 U.S.C. § 1651.

In essence, the "Writ of Error Coram Nobis" acts as an assurance that the deserved relief will not be denied as a result of technical limitations of other post-conviction remedies such as the "custody" requirement under 28 U.S.C. § 2255.

When a court without jurisdiction convicts and sentences a defendant, the conviction and sentence are void from their inception and remain void long after a defendant has fully suffered their direct force. Moreover, as the Supreme Court reiterated in Spencer v. Kemna, 523 U.S. 1 (1998), "it is a obvious fact of life that most criminal convictions do entail adverse legal consequences." id. At 512-13. As noted in United States v. Morgan, 346 U.S. 502 (1954), Coram Nobis relief is available after the sentence has been served because "the results of the conviction may persist, Subsequent convictions may carry heavier penalties, civil rights may be affected." id. at 512-13. "The demands of the Constitution as envisaged by this court, have moved federal and state courts to acknowledge that due process requires corrective judicial process in the nature of Coram Nobis be available to expunge a void judgment when all other avenues of judicial relief are unavailable. " id. Morgan.

A successful petition for issuance of a "Writ of Error Coram Nobis" is found in United States v. Peter, 310 F.3d 709 (11th Cir. 2002).

In Peter, after the defendant had completed his sentence (including his supervised release), a Supreme Court decision was issued that conclusively established that the specific acts he had admitted to in entering his guilty plea did not constitute a criminal offense. The Eleventh Circuit Court of Appeals found this claim to meet the definition of a jurisdictional defect and decided that it could not be waived and that the continuing effect of a felony guilty plea kept the issue from being moot. A "Writ of Error Coram Nobis" was found to be necessary to correct the original judgment that the court never had the power to enter.

No Judicial Immunity

"No judicial process, whatever form it may assume, can have any lawful authority outside of the limits of the jurisdiction of the court or judge by whom it is issued; and an attempt to enforce it beyond these boundaries is nothing less than lawless violence." <u>Ableman v. Booth</u>, 21 Howard 506 (1859).

When a judge knows that he lacks jurisdiction, or acts in the face of clearly valid statutes expressly depriving him of jurisdiction, judicial immunity is lost. See e.g. <u>Rankin v. Howard</u>, 633 F.2d 844 (9th Cir. 1980).

"Asking the ignorant to use the incomprehensible to decide the unknowable."

—Hiller B. Zobel, *'The Jury on Trial' in American Heritage* (1995)

Abbreviations

AEDPA	Antiterrorism and Effective Death Penalty Act
App.	Appendix
Appx.	Appendix
Cert.	Certiorari
Cir.	Circuit
Civ.	Civil
Dist.	District
E.D.	Eastern District
e.g.	for example
esp.	especially
etc.	et cetera
F. or Fed.	Federal
Fla.	Florida

The Seven Ways to Overcome the Federal Statute of Limitations

id.	idem
i.e.	that is
M.D.	Middle District
N.D.	Northern District
No.	number
Okla.	Oklahoma
P. or Proc.	Procedure
Pa.	Pennsylvania
PLRA	Prison Litigation Reform Act
Pub.	Public
R.	Rules
RICO	Racketeer Influenced and Corrupt Organization Act
S.D.	Southern District
S.Ct.	Supreme Court
SMJ	Subject-matter Jurisdiction
Stat.	Statute
U.S.	United States
U.S.C.	United States Code
W.D.	Western District
W.L.	West Law

"Ignorance is an evil weed, which dictators may cultivate among their dupes, but no democracy can afford among its citizens."

—William Henry Beveridge, *Social Insurance and Allied Services (1942)*

Glossary

accrual
: To come into existence as an enforceable claim or right.

All Writs Act
: A federal statute that gives the U.S. Supreme Court and all other courts established by Congress the power to issue writs in aid of their jurisdiction and in conformity with the usages and principles of the law. See e.g. 28 U.S.C. § 1651 (a).

binding precedent
: A precedent that a court must follow. For example, a lower court is bound by an applicable holding of a higher court in the same jurisdiction.

The Seven Ways to Overcome the Federal Statute of Limitations

en banc	[French "on the bench"]. With all judges present and participating; in full court.
free-standing	Standing alone or on its own foundation free of support or any attachment.
in forma pauperis	[Latin "in the manner of a pauper"]. In the manner of an indigent who is permitted to disregard filing fees and court costs.
jurisdiction	A court's power to decide a case or issue a decree.
nullify	The act of making something void.
persuasive precedent	A precedent that is not binding on a court, but that is entitled to respect and careful consideration.
retroactive	Extending in scope or effect to matters that have occurred in the past.
statute of limitations	A law that bars claims after a specific time period.
sua sponte	[Latin "of one's own accord; voluntarily"] Without prompting or suggestion; on its own motion.
supra	[Latin "above"] Earlier in this text; used as a citational signal to refer to previously cited authority.

subject-matter jurisdiction   Jurisdiction over the nature of the case and type of relief sought; the extent to which a court can rule on the conduct of persons or the status of things.

tolling   To stop or interrupt the running of something, esp. a statute of limitations.

void   Something that is of no legal effect; null.

"Love, friendship, respect do not unite people as much as common hatred for something."

—Anton Chekov, *Notebooks* (1921)

Useful Resources

Blackstone Career Institute

Blackstone offers legitimate paralegal courses for affordable prices. They have been around since 1890 and are nationally known and regionally accredited. You can contact them at:

Blackstone Career Institute
P.O. Box 3717 Allentown, PA 18106-0717
www.blackstone.edu

Fairshake Reentry Resource Center

Fairshake offers non-traditional support and information to inmates and ex cons entering back into the community. Through an interactive blend of electronic tools, reentry awareness and community building, Fairshake encourages released prisoners, and all stakeholders, to participate in the successful reintegration of formerly incarcerated people back into society. You can contact them at:

Fairshake Reentry Resource Center
P.O. Box 63 Westby, WI 54667
www.fairshake.net

Prison Inmates

Prison Inmates offers a social network exclusively for inmates, friends, family & those who wish to correspond with them. You can contact them at:

Prison Inmates
P.O. Box 6560
Pahrump, N.V. 89041-6560
www.prisoninmates.com

Prison Legal News

Prison Legal News is a monthly publication that reports on legal cases and news stories related to prisoner rights and conditions of confinement. You can contact them at:

Prison Legal News
P.O. Box 1151
Lake Worth, FL 33460 www.prisonlegalnews.org

Prison Pen Pals

Prison Pen Pals is an award winning pen-pal company that was started in 1996. It claims to be the most visited, largest, and longest running site of its kind on the internet. You can contact them at:

Prison Pen Pals
P.O. Box 235
East Berlin, PA 17316-0235
www.prisonpenpals.com

Write A Prisoner.com

Write A Prisoner.com is one if the largest and highest ranked penpal sites out there. It has been featured on CNN, 20/20, Fox News, Dr. Phil, 0 Magazine, E! True Hollywood, and hundreds of others. You can contact them at:

Write A Prisoner.com
P.O. Box 10 Edgewater, FL 32132
www.writeaprisoner.com

"You might as well try to employ a boa constrictor as a tape measure as to go to a lawyer for legal advice."

—Oliver St. John Gogarty, *Tumbling in the Hay (1939)*

Index